The Fi
Of Incarceration

LESTER YOUNG

Presents

"The 5 stages of Incarceration"

Written by:

Lester Young Jr.

ISBN-13: 9781096717935

FOREWORD

In my many years as a chaplain for the South Carolina Department of Corrections (SCDC), it is common for those who are still incarcerated to talk about their plans to reach out to help others when they are released. They talk about plans to run a halfway house for men leaving prison to successfully transition back to society, help homeless people find housing, or work with youth to keep them from going to prison. What is uncommon, even rare, are those few individuals who reach out to help once they are released. Lester Young is a man that stands at the top of the short list of previously incarcerated men who fulfill the mission of his vision of reaching out and reaching back to make significant contributions to the lives of men and boys at risk of future incarceration. There are several things that make Lester so effective in his mission to help others avoid a life behind the fences of prison; his own prison experience, his passion to lead others into self-transformation, and his program development

3

while incarcerated.

During Lester's years of incarceration, while other men perfected their game of spades, handball or watching Jerry Springer, Lester was educating himself with business classes, cognitive behavior studies, and self-discipline in barriers, boundaries and life choices. For over 5 years, Lester and I worked closely together developing a series of classes in what we called the New Direction portion of SCDC's first character dorm program, <u>Prison to Society</u> (PTS). The classes helped men deal with barriers and boundaries, criminal thinking, risk factors for incarceration, getting out and staying out, giving back, and ultimately Lester's own initiative called "The Five Stages of Incarceration". He lived it, learned it, taught it, and now he is bringing this vital information to the streets to impact as many lives as will listen. He is a man of integrity, wisdom, passion, and vision – a reflection of the life of Ezra the scribe, who studied the law of God, practiced it and then taught it to God's people. –Gerald Potoka

CONTENTS

Chapters	Page

ACKNOWLEDGEMENTS

I most definitely give praise and thanks to God for blessing me to overcome the many struggles I've faced during and after my years of incarceration. Because of God's grace, blessings, and endless mercy, I am the man that I am today.

Thanks to my lovely wife, Felicia Woodberry Young or as I commonly refer to her as "Barakah" (meaning blessing), for believing in me, now and during my years of incarceration. She made sacrifices many years ago to put me in the position to be free. From ordering books, to providing emotional support, not to mention preparing my parole packet, and hiring an incredibly reputable attorney to represent me during my parole hearing, my wife is indeed my accountability partner. Daily she reminds me of the gift that God has bestowed upon me. As of 2018, we've been happily married for eleven years (in which seven of those were while I was serving time in prison). In August of 2015, we were blessed with a beautiful, healthy, active daughter by the name of Kaleeyah Ayanna Young. Indeed, our daughter reminds us of the meaning behind her name, "most bright, shining, beautiful one". Words will never fully express the love I have for them both.

Family is important to any incarcerated individual. Being called for a visit always bought joy to my heart. For many years, my father and sisters travelled religiously to sit with me for 4 hours. God knows we've encountered our "ups" and "downs", but no matter what, they **NEVER** gave up on me. Even though I was physically absent from their lives, I could always depend on emotional, mental, and spiritual support. The love from them is what motivated me to never give up on myself and my life upon release. I made a promise to each of them that I'd make them proud, and with every fiber of my soul I pray that I have. *I love you guys more than you'll ever know!!*

Everyone has that "true" friend that's with you from the beginning to the end. God has blessed me with many, but I'll always remember the words *Frederick Chisolm* said to me from day one of my sentence, *"Brother as long as I eat out here, you're going to eat in there."* This man kept his word and made sure that I had everything I needed to survive. Our friendship is one that has lasted over the years, and I'm forever indebted to him for truly displaying the ultimate meaning of the word "friend".

David Brown was the man I looked up to while I was involved in the drug game. During that time, he was the one you talked with for advice of the "streets". I think David was sent to prison a year or so prior to me. I vaguely remember our first encounter in prison. Needless to say, he was NOT the same person I'd met from the block. David and I engaged in conversations about God, his interest of reading various books (especially learning the dictionary to enhance his vocabulary), and how he committed to making a change in his life. Listening to his words of wisdom gave me the image of what "change" would look like on me. Just as he did on the outside, he began pouring into me all the positive changes he'd made in his life. Although he presented a good case, I wasn't mentally ready to let go of what I'd grown accustomed to. Looking back on those days, I can now appreciate him for wanting better for me. David believed in me more than I believed in myself. In private, I'd reminiscence on his words. Then I visualized the change within myself, and it felt good. Daily, he challenged me to become better than I was the day before. For that, I thank you my brother. I thank you for the words of encouragement that inspired me to be different, as well as MAKE a difference in the lives of others that have and still are serving time.

I encourage everyone to never underestimate the power of volunteers. **Rick Jordan** was a businessman from the community of Charlotte, NC. His business was in Washington, D.C. Rick spent the entire week in Washington. Every weekend, he drove to Charlotte to spend time with his family. I had the privilege of meeting with Rick when he came into the prison as a volunteer. I spoke with him about my interest in wanting to start a business class, and needing someone that could commit to coming in to teach this class. After about an hour or so of talking and getting to know one another, Rick saw the importance of having the class, and he showed no hesitation with driving to Kershaw weekly (every Saturday) to teach this class. He became more than a volunteer, over time I gained a great deal of respect for him. The dedication he showed in preparing me for freedom was like none other. It's a pleasure to have had Mr. Jordan as a mentor during and after prison for the past 4 ½ years. On March 21, 2017, I received a call from Rick's wife informing me that he'd passed away. I was heartbroken and overwhelmed with grief. I pray Rick was proud of me, and happy to know that his lessons are still daily being utilized in my life.

THE FIVE STAGES OF INCARCERATION

Chaplain **Omar Shahid** spent over 20 years coming into various prisons, challenging the Muslim community to think differently. He always encouraged me to think outside of my prison environment and take ownership of my life choices. My respect for him developed as a result of being called out on addressing my own personal anger issues. Actually, he's the inspiration for the second stage of incarceration of "anger". As of today, he remains a faithful mentor. We meet at least every other week for breakfast at **HIS** favorite restaurant located here in Columbia, SC.

I met Chaplain **Gerald Potoka** at Kershaw Correctional during my last 7 years of incarceration. Mr. Potoka recognized my passion to teach and connect with fellow inmates. Thinking back to those days, the thoughts of creating this handbook first came to me under the advisement, supervision and assistance of Chaplain Potoka. Kershaw was the first institution where I was housed and taught "The 5 Stages of Incarceration." Daily, he and I would chat about ways of improving the inmate population. I'm blessed to have had this opportunity to get that one on one mentoring. Out of all the lessons Chaplain Potoka taught, the one I constantly revert back to is "The Law of Reciprocity". For those not familiar with this, it states that in many social situations we pay back what we receive from others. Chap is really passionate about helping others embrace their change of heart. Out of everyone else, he saw my potential and believed in me. Through his teachings I was able to sharpen my skills as a leader, not realizing I was preparing myself for obstacles I'd face after parole. Never will I be able to repay him for the time, support, wisdom and love he's provided (and continues to provide) me with.

I stand on the shoulders of many great men and women that believe in me before, during and after prison. There are *too* many people to individually express appreciation and show gratitude. Please know and understand that I hold each of you dearly within my heart and I pray I never disappoint you. Thanks for years of prayers and support.

"Sow a thought, and you reap an act, sow an act and you reap a habit, sow a habit and you reap a character, sow a character, and you reap a destiny."-Samuel Smiles

INTRODUCTION

When I was 16 years old my life changed drastically after my mother's death. I bought my first drug pack, started hanging out with drug dealers, and smoking marijuana. In just a few months I became a different person. My deepest regret was not saying anything to my mother that morning that I left out for school.

At the age of 19, I was sentenced to serve life in prison (with eligibility of parole **AFTER** serving 20 years). I was denied parole on my first review in 2012. This crushed me, but I didn't allow it to break my spirits. With patience, better strategies, and believing in myself, I was granted parole on May 15, 2014 after serving 22 years and 5 months. During this time, I learned many things about myself as I searched for peace and redemption while adjusting to prison life. Entering the department of corrections at a young age was emotionally intimidating. I lived in a fear of being raped (which was a big thing in the early 1990's), getting stabbed, or being killed. Having these fears made it difficult to focus on anything outside of surviving. This is where having "street smarts" became handy. I had to adapt to my environment and be a fast learner. After learning the "do's" and the "do nots" of prison, I slowly began acclimating to my new surroundings.

The greatest lesson was learning how to distance myself from all negativity. For example, I stopped getting high, I know longer participated in gambling, didn't show interest in visiting the basketball courts, and was strictly particular of the company I wanted to be around, as well as allowed to be around me. By applying these behaviors into my daily regime, I found that I was now able to spend time educating myself. Changing my mindset and making better choices put me in a better position to one day be paroled (even though my first parole date wasn't until 2012 and the chances of being paroled were about 3%).

The more negativity floating around the prison systems, the more misconceptions are perceived. Daily I sat amongst men (once they found out about my sentence) that constantly said things in hopes of breaking my spirit. There conversations were based around sayings such as *"Lifers never get out"*, or *"If I had a life sentence, I would be wilding out"*, and *"you're wasting time studying to receive a GED in hopes of bettering yourself because you'll probably NEVER get out"*. Even though they tried to bring about doubt, I remained calm and firm within my beliefs and dedicated to my studies. I saw many guys become a victim of the prison environment in a negative way because they lost hope in redemption.

I realized quickly I had to maintain discipline and a strong mindset to mentally make it in prison for 20 years. I started investing in books (which was quite a task because I struggled with reading). Growing up, going to school and getting good grades just wasn't the "cool" thing to do. It's safe to say I entered prison probably reading on a 6-grade level. So, my first task was to build my reading skills based off what I'd already learned. As I came across words I didn't know, I'd pick up the dictionary. I practiced the correct pronunciation, learned the definition, and put each word in a sentence. In addition to improving my reading skills, I increased my vocabulary. Teaching and learning from myself, instilled a feeling of pride, and integrity. It was at that moment I realized I had potential to be and do much more.

The next step was improving how I dealt with pinned up emotions. Like many inmates, I struggled with personal issues, and having a life sentence disqualified me from attending lots of programs that would probably have allowed me to become more active. For many years, I remained private and grew more content with keeping people out. The lifestyle I had in the streets caused me to shut down and **not trust anyone**. This mindset became too familiar and I found myself repeating the same pattern in prison, so I decided to think outside of the box. I purchased a notebook from the canteen and made a commitment to daily write my thoughts, feelings, and opinions into a journal. To some, this may not seem as if it's a stress reliever, but it worked for me. Writing my thoughts allowed me to release stress and underlying issues I was carrying around. Reading my thoughts changed my perspective on how I viewed my life, my crime, and my future goals. By consistently logging my thoughts in my journal, I was able to open my eyes to different stages of incarceration. As of today, my journals date back from 1992 to 2014 (the year I was paroled).

Serving a life sentence limits an inmate to many State Funded Programs the prison system offers. This is more of an issue when you're housed within a "Level 3" facility (which is where 95% of inmates serving 20+ years were). In my opinion, these are the absolute worst institutions. There were always problems with correctional officers running late or not coming in at all (which caused shortages). The counselors we were told to talk with were drained from working caseloads that eventually became so overwhelming, they had little time to assist inmates with the emotional, mental, psychological, or spiritual guidance they needed and required (especially when you're in a population consisting of at least 1100 men convicted of all kinds of crimes). Many inmates suffered in silence due to lack of interest from caseworkers and continued soothing themselves in a way that was familiar, they stored their feelings (along with everything else) and chose to rebel. Over my years of incarceration and moving from prison to prison, I gained lots of respect. One day I decided to get a group of guys together and share with each of them things I was doing to help maintain my state of peace. I talked about my **five stages of incarceration** in hopes of them acknowledging similar stages going on within themselves. To my surprise, our sessions helped more than any counseling session ever could. These men (that were once nonchalant, angry and extremely disgruntled men) slowly began to open up and talk about their past and present issues. I was able to get through to them and I think it's because the teachings came from one of their own, an incarcerated "lifer" that could relate to their every emotion. Never did I believe I could help or uniquely impact someone enough to recognize their own destructive patterns of crime that paved their path to prison.

The concept of "The 5 Stages of Incarceration" became my framework of self-empowerment and helped me with personal development. As I embraced each phase, I understood the impact of my crime, the void and shame I placed on my family, and the hurt I bought about within my community. I became a better man, a better person and learned to accept ownership for the choices that once molded my way of thinking. Now, even though the chances of being paroled were 3%, I was mentally prepared to face this chance once the opportunity presented itself. I'm blessed that I was able to find my "path to redemption" during my time of incarceration.

INTRODUCTION EXERCISES:

Before you begin reading about the different stages of incarceration, I've created a few exercises to assist with your studies. Remember that as you're reading this information, it's important to be honest with yourself. It doesn't matter what others think, so please don't feel the need to be concerned with their thoughts or opinions. Being inside of prison, I've witnessed firsthand how often individuals allow the opinions of others to hinder them from making a change. Do know and understand that if you're an individual that's bothered by opinions of others, this workbook **WILL NOT** be of ANY assistance to you. While beginning to understand your five stages of incarceration, you must remove yourself from negativity, take accountability for your actions, and then have a "change of heart". One of my favorite sayings (that still rings true to this day) is "association brings assimilation". While studying this workbook, limit conversations with anyone that doesn't support your efforts to bring about a change. Surround yourself with others displaying positive vibes and also searching for a path to redemption.

Here are a few exercises:

1. Get a mirror and stare into it for a few minutes. Write down in your journal YOUR thoughts of the person you see looking back at you.

"The eyes are the windows to your soul" ...

This exercise is one step to helping you see the TRUE YOU, and not the version YOU portray to others

2. For one week, set aside some time in which you can sit alone in a quiet place and practice breathing. Slowly focus on something that means a lot to you.

"In life, some steps need to be taken alone, it's the only way you'll truly understand where you need to go and who you need to be"

It's important to block out unnecessary chatter and listen to your inner voice (conscious). Do you recognize that voice? It's the same voice you heard that spoke against you committing the crime that led you to prison. Continue listening to this voice as this will become your personal navigation towards change.

3. Write a personal letter to yourself listing the things you need to do in order to become a better you (despite how long you're incarcerated).

"Be careful of what you speak into existence, you could be creating your own destruction"

See your time in prison as a blessing rather than a punishment. Walk and talk positive things going forward to motivate your willingness and commitment to change.

4. Grab 2 sheets of paper. On the 1st sheet, write down a list of "friends" you associate with daily (inside your dorm and out). On the back of the 1st sheet, list positive benefits each person has to offer, and on the front of the 2nd sheet, list the bad or negative qualities these people display, then on the back of the 2nd sheet, begin your process of elimination.

"Association brings assimilation"

If someone's good traits outweigh their bad, then this is the person you want in your corner for moral support and to hold you accountable. In the event their bad outweighs their good, then begin your process of elimination. Misery loves company and if you're moving forward their fears and doubts will hold you back.

These are just a few exercises that will warm you up and get your mind right before continuing to read this workbook. **PLEASE DO NOT** rush through the book, it's not a novel. It's a life altering workbook that requires your patience. As you read each chapter, make sure to give 100% to each exercise. This is the only way you'll gain the benefit from this workbook and embrace the new you.

TWO LEVELS OF PRISON ENVIRONMENT

Prison is a gloomy place that can literally destroy an individual emotionally, mentally, spiritually and psychologically. Before exploring the stages of incarceration, it's essential that you understand the 2 levels of the prison environment:

1. First Level: <u>Recriminalization</u> – This happens when the crime is repeated or new ways to commit crimes are learned from other prisoners. Ever heard the saying "an idol mind is the devil's playground"? Level one fits the type person that doesn't see anything wrong with their behavior and is basically upset they were caught. During this moment, they're either thinking of ways to perfect their crime or eagerly searching for new crimes to commit? They conveniently place themselves around others listening to what crime that person committed and begin thinking… *"How am I going to do this again without getting caught"*, or *"I can easily do what they did, and not get caught".*

2. Second Level: <u>Decriminalization</u> – This level is where one acknowledges their criminal thinking and behavior that led to incarceration. Once this level is reached, the individual is adamant about changing the old habits of criminal thinking and behavior. The utilization of their time now becomes a quest for knowledge consisting of bettering themselves and focusing on ways of leading a productive life after prison.

Steps of decriminalization:

1. Stop wasting time engaging in conversations involving anything illegal.
2. Choose reading material that speaks about change and ways to become a better person.

3. Using this workbook, create your own study group (of like minds) within the dorm and remind everyone to be the others accountability partner.

Remember change isn't an easy road to travel, it's a road filled with many valleys of "highs" and "lows", tests, and temptations designed to keep you from becoming a better person. It's a constant battle with the old you. In this process you can't allow frustration to defeat you. Change is all about creating new habits in your life that will assist you in breaking familiar patterns of criminal thinking and behavior.

Bad habits are formed over a course of time. They shape our mindset, our choices and most definitely our behavior. We tend to think it's something we can easily "not do" if we choose not to when in actuality, we've found ways to increase that behavior and that's **probably** the reason that led to your incarceration. These bad habits have to be uprooted in order for new seeds to be planted. Now you can begin the process known as **transformation**.

What are Habits?

"Nothing so needs reforming as other people's habits."
-Mark Twain

Webster Dictionary defines habit as:

(a) Usual way of behaving;

(b) A way of acting or doing that has become fixed by repeated occurrences;

(c) Characteristic way of growing.

"People don't decide their future, they decide their habits and their habits decide their future."-John Maxwell

According to an article by James Clear (Behavioral Psychology), "On average it takes more than 2 months before a new behavior becomes automatic, 66 days to be exact. And how long it takes a new habit to form can vary widely depending on the behavior, the person and the circumstances."

During my time in prison, I was amazed once I acknowledged how my past habits became second nature to me and became a part of my daily choices that led to criminal activity, which opened the door for me being sentenced to prison. This workbook is all about acknowledging your habits that shaped your choices. Familiarize yourself with habits now, and how they impact your choices. In later reading you'll have exercises designed to challenge your way of thinking and discuss how your habits cause you to see yourself.

Exercise on Habits

List 5 Bad habits that you need to change.

1.

2

3.

4.

5.

List 5 Good habits that you want to create in your life

1.

2.

3.

4.

5.

"We are what we repeatedly do. Success is not an action but a habit." Aristotle

STAGE ONE OF INCARCERATION

"SELF-DENIAL"

"The secret of change is to focus all of your energy, not on fighting the old, but on building the new." -Socrates

What is the meaning of Self-Denial? It's the unwillingness to address or acknowledge core issues that affect your decision, behavior, and choices. Hopefully you're at a point in life in which you're willing to change some things that went into shaping your thinking and behavior. Every individual has the key to unlocking the doors of the past. Being that this chapter is "self-denial it's common for one to cover up this particular area while in prison.

It took me a few years to realize this one little thing, "**NO** one or **NOBODY**" can release me from my own prison but me! Once I started focusing my energy inwardly, I was able to understand what happened in my life prior to prison is what bought about my actions. Honestly speaking, I can't deny that the battle of walking away from who I was, to groom the man I strived to be was extremely difficult. I'd developed so many habits to cover and dismiss the core reasons for my behavior that I had know idea of how to differentiate **what was right**, **what was wrong**, or **what I'd told myself was right or wrong**. All I knew, at that time, is committing and getting away with crime was not only a quick come up, but was cool. I'm sure you can relate. This is where I started writing down my thoughts in a journal each day after taking a few hours out for deep thought and prayer. This process took some time for me to practice. Like many people, some of the things in my past were painful and I'm willing to bet that you will commit to reading this workbook and within a few days, you'll stop.

This workbook will challenge you to be honest with yourself by opening painful doors from your past, and inspire you to create new habits. Your comfort zone will be a little shaken and cause you to find random excuses to stop and give up on this process. I bet you're asking yourself… "How does he know this"? It's because I too have struggled with this. It goes back to having an idol mind. Sometimes we tend to entertain ALL the wrong things when we're bored. Once the thought of being positive and productive surfaces within our thoughts, we find a way to block it and go back to what we know. Since being a teenager, I would start a project and within a few days, I'd quit. This was indeed a bad habit that I knew I had to change.

The following list describes some things I was in "self-denial" about:

1. ***Low self-esteem***- I never cared for my appearance. This made it easy for me to target others before they targeted me. I lacked confidence, so my way of accommodating (for what I saw to be a short coming) was shopping for clothes and shoes. It's crazy but in my mind, it covered up my weaknesses from the outside world. Attention is what I craved (which is why the idea of getting in trouble in school, smoking marijuana, selling drugs, going to shock prevention classes, and being known as the "neighborhood bad boy" was a good look for me).

2. **Grief**- The loss of a parent is troubling for anyone, regardless of age. As a teenager, it was hard for me to process losing my mother. I never got the chance to apologize to her for an argument we had the night before she passed away. I grieved my mother's death for 9 years or more, it still pains me to this day, but I've learned how to deal with it better over the past few years of being home. I wasn't able to correctly articulate my pain to my father, sisters or family members. Therefore, I internalized this pain which shaped my behavior and made it easier for me to project an "I don't care about anyone or anything attitude." Also opening the doors to an active lifestyle of destruction.

>*When you don't have a healthy outlet to speak about your grief, you act out in many ways. My most valuable tool was writing in my journal. This allowed me the freedom I needed to openly express myself without being judged or viewed by the population as being weak. So, if you haven't started journaling yet... **PLEASE STOP HERE** and log your thoughts! You'll be glad you did later*

3. **Guilt**- I had no idea that at some point, **before and during incarceration**, I was going to hit a huge wall of self-guilt. Once the realization that someone died as a result of my actions, and now I'm really in prison for the next 20 years (with the possibility of parole) hit me, I felt the largest knot in my throat.

24

For about 3 years, I battled with different emotions of guilt. Someone is still grieving the loss of their family member, and once again I let down my family. Depression kicked in, causing me to cling to myself (and my room) for days. I couldn't talk with anyone, not even my roommate. In prison, when you open up and share your emotions that shows a sign of weakness. At this time, I'd only been in prison a few years; the last thing I was going to show anybody is I was "weak". So all I could do was lay in bed hiding under the covers filled with guilt

I taught the materials for this workbook to others while I was incarcerated on different yards and learned more core issues regarding self-denial. A lot of guys never understood that they too were experiencing the same or similar issues involving their stage of self-denial.

Listed below are core behaviors most people affiliate to self-denial:

1. *Abuse*~ commonly defined as to misuse, to bad effect or for a bad purpose. There are 3 types of abuse:

> a. *Physical* - any act intentionally committed to causing injury or trauma to another person.

> b. *Emotional*- consists of criticism, intimidation and manipulation.

> c. *Sexual*- refers to molestation, and usually involves undesired sexual behavior by one person upon another.

2. *Addiction*~ the fact or condition of being addicted to a particular substance, thing or activity. There are 2 types of addiction:

a. **Substance** (alcohol/drug) - a progressive, relapsing condition that is characterized by compulsive alcohol or drug use. Although substance use may be the activity most commonly associated with addiction, a person is capable of developing an addiction to certain behavioral addictions as well.

b. **Behavioral** or **Process** (gambling, eating, pornography) –is when a person essentially becomes dependent on the pleasurable feelings that certain behaviors bring, and begins to compulsively act out that behavior to reach that high over and over again.

3. **Abandonment Issues**~ typically stems from childhood loss (losing a parent rather it's through death or divorce) or inadequate physical or emotional care.

4. **Grief**~ a deep sorrow (especially when caused by someone's death or any other type bad news) that comes in the following stages:

a. **Shock**~ immediate reaction upon hearing bad news
b. **Denial**~ preventing the inevitable
c. **Anger**~ having to deal with pinned up emotions
d. **Bargaining**~ compromising to find a way out
e. **Depression**~ beginning to acknowledge the inevitable
f. **Testing**~ looking for other possible solutions
g. **Acceptance**~ finally coming to terms with the situation

5. **Guilt**~ feeling of responsibility or remorse for some offense, crime, wrong doing (rather real or imaginary).

6. **Criminal Thinking**~ is present in each of us to varying degrees, but more prevalent within our society.

Now that you've been introduced to some reasons of self-denial, let's practice some exercises to apply what you've learned and know about yourself thus far.

In each exercise, read my personal narrative and how I dealt with stages of my incarceration.

Abuse/Abandonment

- *Personal Narrative~* I suffered with emotional abuse. My father was an active part of my life, but he neglected to provide the attention I required in my adolescent life. Dad shut down on my sisters and I after my mom passed away. This led to him becoming difficult to converse with. When I did go to school, I played sports in hopes of our bond strengthening, but I'd always get disappointed when he never showed up. I noticed the more trouble I got into, the more attention I received from him. Dad frequently made remarks on how I'd end up in jail or prison if I continued on the path I was on.

1) Did you suffer any form of abuse or abandonment from your parents or guardian? If so, define the category from the list that your abuse falls into and describe how you dealt with this growing up.

_____
_____
_____

2) Do you think this form of abuse impacted your life? If so, how did it impact your thinking?

_____
_____
_____

3) Have you addressed these issues of abuse? If not, how are you dealing with them?

_____
_____
_____

4) Have you confronted your abuser or the individual that abandoned you?

_____
_____
_____

Addiction:

- ***Personal Narrative:*** At age 16, I began experimenting with smoking marijuana in hopes of numbing emotions/feelings that I wasn't ready to deal with. Of course this was a temporary fix, but for the time I was engaged in it, it did what I sought out for it to do. The night that led to my life sentence started with me being heavily intoxicated on marijuana and alcohol. The mixture of these 2 substances boosted my ego and encouraged my "don't care" attitude.

1) Did you have any addictions prior to your incarceration? If, so list your addiction(s):

   _____

   _____

2) Do you consider yourself an addict? Rather you answer yes or no, please explain the reasoning behind your answer:

   _____

   _____

   _____

   _____

3) If you answer yes to question 2, List what you're doing now to get help with this (or these) issues.

   _____

   _____

   _____

   _____

4) How do you plan to continue dealing with this (or these) issue(s) upon release?

   _____

   _____

   _____

   _____

5) List five ways your addiction has impacted your life and those you love:

_____

_____

_____

_____

Grief and Self- Guilt:

"Guilt upon the conscience, like rust upon the iron, both defiles and consumes it, gnawing and creeping into it, as that does which at last eats out the very heart and substance of the mental."
– Robert South

- *Personal Narrative:* The night prior to my mother's passing; she and I had an argument about me washing dishes. It didn't end well. I slept with that anger through the night and carried it with me into the dawn of the next day. My dad asked that I stay home from school to take care of her until he came home on his lunch break to take her to her doctor's appointment. I told him **"No"** and that I wanted to go to school. I knew she was lying in bed not feeling her best because of flu-like symptoms, but I couldn't move past our disagreement from the night prior. Shortly after being in school only a few hours, I was called to the office. I wasn't at all prepared to hear the words "your mother has passed away". I felt dumbfounded and a tad confused. My heart raced, my jaw dropped, and I was overwhelmed with sadness mixed with numbness. For a long time I remained quiet, I just couldn't find the words to express the way I was feeling. Even at (and after the) funeral, I remained nonchalant and in a complete state of denial. I never spoke to anyone about my grief and feelings of guilt. Once the realization that my mom, the rock of our family, the one that nurtured me, the one that made sure we were good and happy, and the one I knew supported me was physically gone from this world, I instantly became angry and rebelled against any and every one in a position of authority. Starting with my father, then my teachers, principals and most definitely law enforcement.

1) Have you lost a loved one (before or during incarceration) and still dealing with the grief of it?

_____

_____

_____

_____

2) If your answer is yes, then list ways you think you can finally address this loss and move forward:

_____

_____

_____

_____

3) Do you think your use of drugs/alcohol, anger issues, and engaging in criminal activities, was a way of numbing your pain of grief and guilt? *Explain your answer and remember to be honest, this is a step in aiding with your own personal healing*

_____

_____

_____

_____

_____

4) In your opinion, are you emotionally living a healthier life? If your answer is yes then list 5 things you've done (or are currently doing) in order to continue fulfilling this lifestyle. If no, then list 5 ways you can start living this lifestyle:

_____

_____

_____

_____

_____

_____

THE FIVE STAGES OF INCARCERATION

Criminal Thinking:

It's important for individuals to understand you don't just wake up one morning and decide it's a good day to commit a crime. There's a process that takes place in shaping your thoughts, behaviors, and choices. This comes from the different influences that took place over a period of time impacting your perception of life in some type of way. The thoughts of criminal activity became enticing, cool and gave you a form of power. You began plotting and planning the crime(s) with ambition and determination, because that thrust of power catered to your ego and convinced you of one thing and one thing only, "I'm not going to get caught". I call this "The Grooming Process"

Movies and Music:
a. create false perceptions
b. appeal to your desires
c. form a false concept
d. can influence
e. encourages behavior (positive or negative)

Environment:
a. your community (especially one considered in poverty)
b. lack of education
c. dysfunctional family structure

Partners and Friends:
a. living up to their image
b. following their patterns
c. looking for approval
d. wanting acceptance

1. What movies/songs shaped your criminal thinking, behavior, and choices that led to prison?

_____

_____

_____

_____

2. What other influences do you believe went into shaping your
    path that led to your criminal thinking?

    _____

    _____

    _____

    _____

3. How did poverty, family dysfunctionality, and abuse affect your
    decision-making process prior to committing your crime and
    incarceration?

    _____

    _____

    _____

    _____

4. What kind of criminal activities did you witness in your
    community growing up that played a role in shaping your
    criminal thinking?

    _____

    _____

    _____

    _____

5. List 3 childhood "friends" and write rather they were a positive
    or negative influence in your childhood:

    _____

    _____

    _____

6. If you listed any negative influences, did they play a role in your
    crime and do you still associate with them?

    _____

    _____

THE FIVE STAGES OF INCARCERATION

The thought process of criminal thinking consists of:

- Refusing to take responsibility for one's behavior, decision making, actions, and reasoning of jail time or prison;
- Always trying to manipulate others, the system and even the process of change;
- Believing you're invincible, unique and above the law;
- Rebellious, risk taker and feeling justified in committing a crime not carrying about the harm it brings to others.

The 3 forms of the grooming process shape the criminal thinking. It's important that you correct this criminal thinking now rather than later. I've come across many people whom have maxed out, or been paroled and return back to prison because they continued the same patterns and stayed within the lines of being groomed by the same processes as before.

In this stage of incarceration, I have pointed out a few things that most individuals incarcerated are in self-denial about. You have to focus on addressing these different areas. Whatever your reason is, be it abuse, addiction(s), grief, guilt, abandonment issues, or suffering from the stages of the grooming process, continue on this journey to redemption. Face your fears, become the person you need to be. Not for your spouse, your children, your peers or your community… become the person you need to be for yourself, and then everything else will fall into place. Trust me, I'm talking to your from my own experience of once being in the place you are now.

Before entering "Stage 2", make sure you've completed ALL of the exercises for "Stage 1" and I can't stress to you enough to remain loyal to writing daily in your journal.

"A journey of a thousand miles begins with a single step." ~Lao-Tzu

STAGE TWO OF INCARCERATION

"ANGER"

"Anger doesn't solve anything it builds nothing, but it can destroy everything." –Roy T. Bennett

While dealing with anger there's a lack of remorse, accountability, and empathy for those whom have been impacted by your actions. Anger is a mixture of fear, shame, and hurt sometimes fueled with issues of betrayal, abandonment, abuse, lack of self-worth and rejection. Some studies have stated most of our anger stems from unresolved issues that were never addressed during childhood or adolescent years. Without the **proper counseling**, anger will pass on into your adult years causing lots of chaos and turmoil.

The four most common forms of anger:

1. ***Direct:*** Anger towards the one that inflicted the pain or injury.
2. ***Indirect:*** Victimizing others for the pain or injury someone has caused you to experience.
3. ***Unresolved:*** Resentment, bitterness, and rage towards the person that caused the pain or injury.
4. ***Inward:*** Comes from shame, guilt of abuse, abandonment, betrayal, and rejection.

When there is a lack of understanding and awareness these forms of anger play an important role in shaping one's mindset, behavior, choices, and self-perception. They also play a critical role in the commission of one's crime. You will notice inside the prison environment there are a lot of angry individuals displaying 1 (if not all 4) form of anger. The aura of prison isn't pleasant, so it's easy for someone to absorb **MORE** bitterness, **MORE** brokenness, **MORE** issues of abandonment, and **MORE** hurt. Before long a monster begins growing within and the right situation will open the door to destruction.

Anger:

"Don't waste your time in anger, regrets, worries, and grudges. Life is too short to be unhappy."-Roy T. Bennett

- *Personal Narrative:* I admit my first few years were filled with all 4 forms anger. Daily, I waited for someone (anyone) to give me a reason to lash out. This is where my mentor **Omar Shahid** greatly impacted my life. I was in an Islamic class one evening and his question to the Muslim population was "Why were we so angry"? My response was one that didn't sit well with him; I stated what I felt to be the obvious and replied… "We're not being treated fairly by the prison administration of how we justify our anger". His response was… "You are angry with the wrong people". Now keep in mind I was still prematurely young in my thinking so of course, I felt his reply didn't accurately define what I was looking for. The more he spoke about the reasoning's of anger the more it made sense to me. Chaplain Shahid shared 4 common reasons men incarcerated are angry:

- *God*
- *Parents*
- *Peers/Friends*
- *Yourself*

I was **directly** angry with God for taking my mother away, I had **unresolved** anger towards my father for not giving me the time and attention I needed after my mother passed away, I was **indirectly** angry with my friend that sided with the State and testified against me, and lastly, I was **inwardly** angry with myself for shame I bought to my family, the embarrassment of my crime, and the rejection I received from peers while growing up.

From that class I understood why it was hard to connect with finding myself spiritually, God doesn't come into any heart filled with anger. He can't comfortably reside there. In order to receive inner peace and salvation, I had to make peace with God. I slowly started working on the core things that was causing my anger. Having my foundation based around God was essential to my life. There was absolutely no way I was going to serve a life sentence without being able to talk to, or rely on God. The choice then became obvious, anger had no place in my life and I was determined not to be the typical, bitter inmate claiming to have found God in prison and forget about Him after release. My faith was important to me then and even more now since being free.

Anger Exercise:

1. Describe your anger in the past and present:

   _____
   _____
   _____
   _____

2. Is your incarceration a result of your anger?

   _____
   _____
   _____
   _____

3. Of the 4 forms of anger, which do you associate more with and why:

   _____
   _____
   _____
   _____

4. How can you gain control of your anger at this point in your life?

5. In what way did your family, community, or environment shape the way you deal with anger?

This stage of incarceration is very imperative to the process of growth. As long as anger resides within or can easily take over, then your change will become more and more difficult to embrace. Remember God doesn't come into the heart that's filled with bitterness, anger, and rage. As you move from chapter to chapter be mindful that you have to keep working to better your life. This will only come about through prayer and perseverance.

Before entering "Stage 3", make sure you've completed ALL of the exercises for "Stage 2" and once again, remain loyal to writing daily in your journal.

STAGE THREE OF INCARCERATION

"VICTIMIZATION"

This prevents the individual from taking ownership or responsibility for their actions. It's common talk in prison to hear individuals claiming to be victims of their crime. Also known as **"The Blame Game"**, this stage enables those incarcerated to continue an ongoing cycle of justifying their criminal thinking and behavior and adds more difficulty for change.

LISTED BELOW ARE THE COMMON REASONS WE DEFINE OURSELVES AS VICTIMS:

- Race
- Poverty
- Single Parent Home
- **THE SYSTEM**
- Lack of Education
- Lack of opportunities

Unlike self-denial, and anger, victimization feeds your ego, but it prevents growth. You feel no **empathy** (ability to understand feelings of others) or **apathy** (lack of interest or concern) for anyone outside of yourself. As long as it's someone else's fought "you did this" or "you had to do that" then you'll never realize this ongoing cycle leads to recidivism and recriminalization. The longer you engage yourself in conversation with others in which you view yourself as the victim, the easier it becomes to not remember there actually is (or was) a victim. There is very little (if any) conversation in regards to the actual victim(s) that has been impacted. During my first years of teaching, many guys shared how they purposely blocked out events of their crime. For many, this goes back to what I shared earlier in reference to showing weakness; they weren't emotionally stable to address the details of the crime, so they pushed it away… promising to deal with the issues later. Every crime committed in the community or the society at large has a direct or indirect ripple effect.

VICTIMIZATION:

- *Personal Narrative*: I walked into the court room filled with arrogance and totally prepared to be released after my trial. I was innocent and a victim of the system. Yes, his family was there, but I didn't care. The murder was justified. Had he not tried to rob my homeboy then this never would have happened~ right? Why did the judge sentence me to "Life in Prison with the possibility of parole after serving 20 years?" This was the end result of what some might call a "drug deal gone badly". While thinking back to the court date, I would occasionally laugh to myself thinking, "These people are crazy". Even though I'd been practicing my religion, and regularly praying, I was still content with being the victim. How was I able to think this way you ask? Well as long as you remain emotionally and mentally within your comfort zone, then spiritually you're not growing. This is criminal thinking and becomes common in prison. I knew I could no longer live this way. I prayed asking for forgiveness and help with learning to atone for my actions. Have you heard that in prayer, be very careful and specific of what you ask? God will definitely listen to the heart of believers seeking answers. One night while watching television, I heard the pain in the voice of a grieving mother whom had recently dealt with the murder of her child. I remember lying on my bed, then turning over on my back with tears in my eyes. It was at that moment I accepted responsibility for the murder and acknowledged the feelings of the victim and his family.

THE FIVE STAGES OF INCARCERATION

Victimization/Blame Game Exercise:

1) Do you view yourself as the victim of the crime that was committed? Rather you answer yes or no, explain:

_____

_____

_____

2) Have you accepted responsibility for your behavior and the choices that led to harming someone directly or indirectly by your crime?

_____

_____

_____

3) Do you have any remorse for the crime committed? Explain:

_____

_____

_____

4) Do you have any remorse for the crime that you are incarcerated for? Explain:

_____

_____

_____

5) Have you mentally blocked out your crime, for your victim(s) to help you cope with your time?

_____

_____

6) Are you ready to take responsibility for the actions that led to your incarceration? If yes, what steps are you taking outside of reading this workbook?

_____

_____

_____

_____

_____

True change can only emerge from taking ownership of the choices and behavior that led to prison. Victimization has to be addressed early on. Until you realize this, you're in a strong sense of denial therefore preparing yourself to be recriminalized. Look back to the Introduction as I spoke about Recriminalization and Decriminalization.

Before entering "Stage 4", make sure you've completed ALL of the exercises for "Stage 3" and remember… record your emotions **DAILY** in your journal.

"Work hard for what you want because it won't come to you without a fight. You have to be strong and courageous and know that you can do anything you put your mind to. If somebody puts you down or criticizes you, just keep on believing in yourself and turn it into something positive." -Leah LaBelle

STAGE FOUR OF INCARCERATION

"FORGIVENESS"

"All men make mistakes but only wise men learn from their mistakes."-Winston Churchill

Forgiveness is a powerful emotion that empowers someone to move past the hurt, pain, guilt, and brokenness. This stage is all about moving forward in your life and letting go of things that have been preventing you from moving forward. The heart is a vessel that shouldn't be consumed with bitterness or resent. To forgive brings joy and relief to the heart that has been trained to not feel remorse.

Four phases of forgiveness:

1. *Seeking forgiveness from God:* Before asking forgiveness from others you must first seek forgiveness from God. This makes the process easier because God will definitely aid the heart in repentance and forgiveness.
2. *Seeking forgiveness for you:* After seeking forgiveness from God, you must then forgive yourself. Forgiveness is for you and carrying around anger and hatred causes stress that often leads to sickness, physically and emotionally.
3. *Seeking forgiveness from those you have harmed:* Depending upon the action, remember some people can carry grudges for an eternity. As you request forgiveness place yourself in their position and realize the pain may still greatly impact them. Make sure to display sincere concern when requesting forgiveness.
4. *Forgiving those whom have harmed you:* Adults are always responsible for their own behavior. Just remember the individual(s) that caused you harm may have been a victim at one point in their life.

FORGIVENESS

- ***Personal Narrative:*** Part of my journey to finding a better me and healing from the pain I carried into prison and while I was in prison was finding forgiveness for my friend that testified against me. In addition to him, I harbored unresolved anger towards a few individuals that I told myself I'd never be able to forgive on any terms. However, I committed myself to practicing Islam (being Muslim) and tried to live a better life in spite of my environment. Part of the Islamic faith is that you pray five times a day, fast during the month of Ramadan for 30 days, read the Holy Quran and stay away from any kind of intoxication. During the month of Ramadan in 1996, I was at Allendale Correctional Institution. The prison was on lockdown due to a riot, so I wasn't able to leave my room to break the fast. I decided to lie down and utilize this time to focus on my growth. At that moment, something came over me about forgiveness for those whom have hurt me. I came to the realization that I wasn't growing spiritually ever since I was found guilty. Instantly, I got a little bothered as thoughts of me being here my friends being out living their lives free of guilt reminded me that I still had not forgiven anyone that I felt betrayed me. It's amazing that I was able to practice everything else of my faith accept finding forgiveness for others and seek forgiveness for those that I hurt. It took a few days to get up and begin this spiritual cleansing of my heart. Finally, I stopped procrastinating, got a piece of paper and wrote down a list of things I had learned about forgiveness. Then I wrote down the names of those I needed to forgive and those I needed to ask for forgiveness.

Seeking Forgiveness from God: I was the one everyone came to for knowledge and advice about Islam, so seeking forgiveness was something I had to do. In the commandment it says, **"Thou Shall not Kill"**. I knew my crime was a great sin in the eyes of God. Therefore, I immediately repented over a dozen or more times for taking a life over something as senseless as drugs. I prayed for forgiveness for lots of things, but this was the first time I seeked repentance from God. Please understand that I'm not at all insinuating the first time I talked with God in prayer about forgiveness I felt the change happen instantly. As weeks passed I started learning that there were other levels to repentance and seeking forgiveness. Therefore, I started taking the steps to understand the different levels of forgiveness and worked towards them.

Seeking Forgiveness for you: I carried a lot of guilt from the age of 16 until my late 20's. I still blamed myself for not apologizing to my mother before leaving for school the morning she passed away, for leaving my sisters to grow up without their brother to look out for them, bringing shame to my family name and having blood on my hands for killing someone. My worst regret was disappointing my Dad. Had it not been for the power of prayer, these burdens would have broken my spirits causing a relapse of the growth process I was doing so well on. To top it off, I didn't have anyone I could talk to about what was eating at me each day. I started writing down these emotions and coping with them. These emotions turned into me writing myself an apology letter. I felt free and was able to focus on living a positive life. Forgiveness was the key to my personal freedom, my peace of mine, and finding purpose in my darkness.

Seeking Forgiveness from those you have harmed: My pride played a key role in this step. For me to apologize for anything is something I was adamant about **NOT** doing. Every time I tried taking this step, I'd make an excuse as to why I couldn't do it that day. A few days later, I made an intention to try again, but still nothing. I just couldn't find the nerve to show weakness. God will always give you what you ask when your heart is sincere. I didn't leave the room so this night he came to me through television again. Indeed God has a funny sense of humor and shows up when he's needed the most. Remember the show Dateline? There was an episode in reference to different crimes committed in which the victim(s) spoke out on how the crime had impacted them. Even though it was hard for each of them to express, they were still able to speak about their loved one that had been taken away as a result of murder. My first instinct was to change the channel, but I heard that inner voice saying, "No you need to hear this and feel the pain of the victims". The more I listened, the more my eyes filled with tears and my heart began to hurt from the pain of hearing the victim(s) talk.

This was my sign to put down my pride and seek a way to apologize to those I had hurt. For the first time since the shooting, I had to take ownership for his death. Finally I said my victim's name. I often referred to him as **"that guy"** or **"the dude I killed"**. That night I got out of my bed and sat on the floor praying. Then I was able to do it, I whispered my victim's full name. I sat on the floor for hours crying and begging for his forgiveness. In honor of his name, I made a promise to him that I would not live that kind of lifestyle ever again. The conversation was so deep and emotional, that I'd totally forgotten my roommate was in the room until he said my name and asked if I was okay. I said, "Yes brother, I'm just making peace with my victim tonight". I cried for hours that night.

46

Afterwards, I felt a sense of peace. From that moment, I was competent of enduring any and everything life had in store for me. In addition to making peace with my victim, I felt compelled to seek forgiveness from his family by writing a letter apologizing for my arrogance on the day of the trial and not considering their grief and loss of their loved one. After writing the letter I made contact with "The Victim Witness Agency" for their assistance in getting the letter to his family, with no intentions of receiving a response. I only wanted to make peace. My dad told me to always be a man in spite of any situation and not look for anything in return. No longer did I view my incarceration as a life sentence. My perception changed and I realized being sent to prison was probably the best thing to happen in my life. It became an institution of higher learning that provided relief and confirmation that everything will be ok.

Forgiving those whom have harmed you: It was my **childhood best friend** that was the State's witness that testified against me. I thought he was selfish to think of clearing himself and accepted whatever plea they sold him. The thing that really hurt is the fact that he didn't tell the truth about the events that led to the murder. I remained true to the code by not snitching. Out of my loyalty to the streets, I sat there and never said anything in regards to the case. I accepted my sentence and vowed that I'd do the time and not discuss the details of the case. Because of that I held resentment in my heart that was planted by a deep seed of anger for him. One day I was reading some more materials on forgiveness and I started taking my transformation seriously. I came across this profound quote on forgiving others:

"Anyone can hold a grudge, but it takes a person with character to forgive. When you forgive, you release yourself from a painful burden. Forgiveness doesn't mean what happened was ok, and it doesn't mean that person should still be welcome in your life. It just means you have made peace with the pain, and are already to let it go." –Unknown

After reading this, I prayed on it for a few weeks, then one morning I jumped up, got something to write with and wrote my best friend a letter letting him know how I felt about the trial, his testimony, and him. Because of my pride, it took me a few more days to actually mail this letter. Once I decided it was time, I mailed the letter with no intentions of hearing back from him. Besides I didn't forgive him for him, I forgave him for me. After a week or so, I was in the room watching television. I saw a letter being slid under the door so I got up to see whom the letter was from. To my surprise it was from my best friend. I hesitated for a while before opening the letter. All types' feelings, thoughts, and unresolved emotions filled my head. What could he possibly have to say to me? So, I opened his letter. It was obvious he'd been looking for a way to get things off of his chest as well. He was under the impression that I'd never speak to him again, so like me, he blocked his feelings and emotions until he could comfortably let them out. He was filled with apologies, regret, and raw emotion. After all these years he'd been punishing himself for what he did (and here I am thinking he was living a guilt free life).Me being sentenced to a life sentence emotionally messed him up. To cope with my absence and his betrayal, his drug usage increased. I was blown away to hear he was also hurting and my letter gave him peace knowing that I'd forgiven him. From there the healing process began for the both of us and we continued staying in touch by writing letters.

Forgiveness Exercise:

1. How is your relationship with God, and have you asked God for forgiveness?

_____

_____

_____

2. Have you forgiven yourself? If so, on a separate sheet of paper, write a letter of apology to yourself and once you complete it. Make it a habit to read this letter to yourself daily until you feel like you've forgiven yourself for the things of the past.

_____

3. If you have a victim(s) related to your crime contact the victim's department and find out the procedures in writing a letter to the victim. Make sure your letter isn't about pointing the finger. Just take ownership and apologize for your wrong.

4. List 5 reasons why you need to apologize and forgive.

_____

_____

_____

_____

_____

5. List 5 reasons why you Love yourself.

_____

_____

_____

_____

_____

6. Explain how reading about the first 4 stages have opened your eyes to your own stages of incarceration:

_____

_____

_____

_____

_____

_____

_____

_____

_____

Before entering "Stage 5", make sure you've completed ALL of the exercises for "Stage 4". Have you logged your thoughts today?

"A man should never be ashamed to own he has been in the wrong, which is but saying... that he is wiser today then he was yesterday." -Alexander Pope

STAGE FIVE OF INCARCERATION

"TRANSFORMATION"

"Yes, your transformation will be hard. Yes, you will feel frightened, messed up and knocked down. Yes, you'll want to stop. Yes, it's the best work you'll ever do." -Robin Sharma

In stage four, I introduced you to the power of forgiveness, and how its tools have been proven to mend relationships. Mentally, before one can transcend to the final stages of incarceration, the seed of change has to be planted firmly within the individual's heart. Transformation is a commitment to change during and after your incarceration. Inside the prison environment you'll hear the following religious statements, "I'm Muslim", "I'm Christian", "I'm a changed person", "I'm changing for my kids", or "I'm changing so I don't ever come back to prison". You may have said some of these things yourself. Transformation requires more than just a statement of the tongue. You're going to be hit with many lows before your release. Depending on how well you deal with stress, these lows may or may not mentally break you down. In most cases, individuals talk the talk of change, but when tested, there true selves come into play. If you haven't reached your full growth potential, the breakdowns could trigger some old habits.

To stay true to the process of transformation it requires the fighter within you to fight 10 times harder to create the habits that will allow you to stay committed. I was knocked down so many times by the circumstances surrounding me. I started this journey knowing there was no turning back. I wasn't going to be that inmate that gave into the system by becoming a negative product. I approached my transformation with a higher level of urgency. I was either going to change or die a mental death. My state of mind was better than that, and I refused to serve my time being mentally dead or what we call institutionalized.

The "Negative" (Institutionalized) Individual Serving Time:

➢ Wastes time daily
➢ Spends hours playing cards, board games or made up prison games
➢ Utilizes criminal thinking by trying to get contraband inside prison
➢ Not working towards bettering themselves
➢ Lack of interest in reading, or learning a different trade
➢ Still engages in patterns that led to incarceration, or learning how to perfect crimes learned from others.

The "Positive" (Transformed) Individual Serving Time:

✓ Invests in beneficial reading material(s) to assist in their growth
✓ Limits pointless conversations with others not appearing to be a positive part of their growth
✓ Utilizes time attending self-help classes offered within the prison
✓ Addresses their 5 Stages of Incarceration and applying exercises they've learned into their transformation.

- ***Personal Narrative:*** "The Autobiography of Malcolm X" written by Alex Haley gave me a roadmap into how Malcolm educated himself through reading, building a strong vocabulary and became a man of change inside of prison. Reading about the man he was prior to the man he became as a result of his incarceration, motivated me to do the things that were needed to reach this level of transformation. Over the course of my 22 years and 5 months, I became a student of knowledge. Which meant I placed education above everything else, I chose buying books over spending money in the prison canteen. Each book I read opened my eyes to an entirely different perspective. Reading allowed my mind to travel different places. I was more and more excited with the turn of each page. I realized my crime doesn't define me, this prison doesn't define me. Prison became my university of higher learning. By educating myself, I was gifted to positively impact the lives of those inside by setting us up to become successful once released back into society. It's never an easy process to focus on change when your surroundings are filled with more odds against you then for you. The thoughts did surface "Why do I Need to Change", but I learned to see the good within a dark environment. I still was able to see the light that inspired me each day to wake up with the intentions of doing something that will get me closer to my goals, maintain a mental sanity and keep believing there will be better days ahead.

During my Stages of Incarceration, I discovered two great things:

1. ***Life purpose:*** The central motivating aims of your life– the reason you get up in the morning. Purpose can guide life decisions, influence behaviors, shape goals, offer a sense of direction and create meaning.
2. ***My God-given gift:*** That was the ability to articulate myself in a way to now influence others, positively. Growing up I never knew I had this gift. I was the shy kid that lacked confidence of speaking in front of large groups. As I continued walking in my purpose my gift was strengthened for the next phase of my life.

Once I discovered the above gifts, I devoted myself to do and be the best that I can be for myself, my family, and everyone in need of assistance. Being a Certified Life Coach helps me to keep individuals requiring assistance with change on a positive path in life. It's sad someone lost their life in order for my full potential to be reached. By journaling daily, getting to know myself, learning from my mistakes (and those of others), truly helped with acknowledging "The 5 Stages of Incarceration".

<u>Transformation Exercise</u>:

1. List some of the obstacles inside the prison environment that you had to overcome to reach transformation.

_____

_____

_____

_____

2. On a separate sheet of paper write down your 1-year plan for maintaining a transformational mindset during and after your incarceration.
3. What is your purpose that has emerged from this experience of incarceration?

_____

_____

_____

_____

4. List 5 steps you've used to bring about change in your life.

_____

_____

_____

_____

_____

5. List 3 things that you value in life and explain how you intend to protect them.

_____

_____

_____

THE FIVE STAGES OF INCARCERATION

Power of Having a Vision Bigger Than Your Prison Number:

A vision is a picture or idea you have in your mind of yourself or anything that you want to happen. A clear vision helps you pursue dreams, achieve goals and briefly gives you a glimpse into your future. You feel much more valuable as a person when you set a vision by daily achieving goals that help turn that vision into a reality. Having a vision bigger than my inmate number was the one thing that motivated me to continue on the path to redemption and not allow the talk of others to destroy my vision. I cannot tell you how many times, I encountered negative talk from various people on various prison yards. I knew my vision was bigger and I had to protect it from all seeds of doubt.

I created a vision board to give life to my vision. A *vision board* is a tool used to help clarify, concentrate and maintain focus on a specific goal. Creating a vision board is not hard at all; you clip pictures from magazines that represent your vision for life and assemble them on a board. Always starting with small goals, for example... if you still have yet to obtain a GED, find a picture representing education (school, book, diploma), clip that and give yourself a deadline of completing that task. This maintains your focus on things that matter, and help you from straying from your goals.

Conclusion

"The 5 stages of Incarceration" is my personal gift to every incarcerated individual. My sincerest prayer is that this book sparks a change in the reader and the prison environment. A change that daily motivates individuals to dig deeper within them to heal old wounds that have gone unaddressed for years. By the time this book is published, I will have been home for almost five years and working on my presentation addressing the parole board for a pardon. I greatly praise God for this journey and the lessons learned along the way. Without his love, mercy, patience and forgiveness this journey probably would have taken a different course. Many people wonder how I have been able to return back to society with a positive outlook on life, goal driven, walking in my purpose each day, sharing my story with others, and using my voice to make a difference for the millions of individuals incarcerated and returning home after incarceration. It's simple, when you commit your life to change and setting an example of change for others to look up to, makes your walk in life one of purpose.

I still believe there's still a lot of work that needs to be done in criminal justice reform and reentry programs. Our society must focus more on restorative justice (helping those that have been impacted by violent crimes) for the offenders and community, and less on punishing. As you can see this book emphasizes healing, something not observed enough in the criminal justice arena, court system, and prisons. There's a saying "Hurt people, hurt people," and I pray this book helps these people to heal. Always remember, there's value in healing from the pains of the past. Use the new tools you've learned with others within your dorm to create study circles to empower each other.

"You and I possess within ourselves at every moment of our lives, under all circumstances, the power to transform the quality of our lives." -Werner Erhard

ABOUT THE AUTHOR

Lester Young, Jr is a native of Hilton Head Island, South Carolina. At the age of 19, Lester was given a life sentence. On May 15, 2014 (22 years and 5 months later), Lester was released on parole. During this time in prison, Lester watched young men coming into prison. The looks on their faces revealed they had no idea how there life was about to change. It was then that he realized his purpose was to be "that" voice to help at-risk youth and decided to invest in changing his life. Entering into prison without an education was indeed a struggle, but he didn't allow this to stop him from educating himself as well as others. With the support of family and friends that always believed in him, Lester was able to obtain his G.E.D and later enroll in Business Management Courses, via mail, as a student of Ashworth College. Lester began drawing attention and constantly rewarded for his interest in helping others. With permission and no hesitation from the warden, Lester along with the prison chaplain began meeting to create templates, outlines, programs, and classes to instruct and mentor fellow inmates. From this, the idea of starting the non-profit organization "Path2Redemption" was born. After his release, the outlines of his programs are still being taught in prisons.

Path2Redemption hosts workshops for at-risk youth and formerly incarcerated individuals needing assistance with their transformation back into society. Now a Certified Life Coach, he talks about the need to dismiss triggers of past behaviors, coping with being home, job preparations, and dealing with letdowns. Lester also sponsors events that help with the homeless population of Columbia by passing out water and snacks during the hot months and during the winter months, he provides hats, socks, sleeping bags and gloves to make sure they maintain staying warm. He works religiously to volunteer wherever and whenever he can be of assistance. Path2Redemption has joined in workshops with *"Love Beyond Bars"* a program founded by *Jenice Green* that works with families to assist children who have parents incarcerated. He was also featured as a guest speaker for Cynthia Hardy's popular radio broadcast and Sunday morning talk show, "Onpoint with Cynthia Hardy". Lester was also an instructor for ***"The Male Achievement Conference"*** hosted by ***Patrick Patterson***.

Lester was employed with Tyson Foods, Inc. for 3 ½ years. After 3 months of employment, he was promoted. Although he was appreciative of the opportunity given by Tyson Foods, Inc., Lester still didn't fill he was doing all he could do. He wanted to provide more for his family. He continued submitting resumes, and as usual, employers continued closing doors providing him with reasons of denial based upon his (now 25-year-old) criminal background. Lester ventured out and created his own job opportunity, he's the proud owner of "Young's Integrity Pressure Washing Services, LLC,".

His years of volunteering, hosting workshops, and being an active voice within his community were recognized by the organization "JustLeadershipUSA". This organization was founded by a formerly incarcerated male that faced a lot of problems with his own transformation into society after serving time in prison. His mission was "to advocate against the unfair treatment of those incarcerated". The organization's goal is to reduce the prison population by 2030. Lester was offered a great job opportunity and he's now a "Statewide Organizer for SC". In this position, he works diligently to change policies and legislation around the issues of employment, housing, and occupational licensing that are denied to those with criminal backgrounds. The campaign is **#WORKINGfuture** and **#BanningtheBox** from applications (jobs, housing).

In addition to "The 5 Stages of Incarceration", you can read a brief description of Lester's life (prior to prison) found in the book "The Trigger" written by Daniel Patinkin.

If you're interested in having Lester for any speaking engagements and would like to arrange a meeting, please feel free to email him at Path2Redemption515@gmail.com. Make sure to reference "Invitation to speak" in the subject line.

Made in the USA
Monee, IL
25 July 2021